Sad Lover Boy

Sad Lover Boy

Kros Dyck
Illustrations by: Kezia Rooke

Copyright © 2021 by Kros Dyck.

Library of Congress Control Number:		2021918883
ISBN:	Softcover	978-1-5434-9812-7
	eBook	978-1-5434-9813-4

All rights reserved. No part of this book may be reproduced or transmitted in any form or by any means, electronic or mechanical, including photocopying, recording, or by any information storage and retrieval system, without permission in writing from the copyright owner.

The views expressed in this work are solely those of the author and do not necessarily reflect the views of the publisher, and the publisher hereby disclaims any responsibility for them.

Any people depicted in stock imagery provided by Getty Images are models, and such images are being used for illustrative purposes only. Certain stock imagery © Getty Images.

Print information available on the last page.

Rev. date: 09/14/2021

To order additional copies of this book, contact:
Xlibris
844-714-8691
www.Xlibris.com
Orders@Xlibris.com
832659

Contents

It's Time (August 29, 2020) 1

Pipe and Typewriter 2

Let me tell you about this journey I'm on 6

A's Ask 8

An Empty Night 9

Love Like Shakespeare 11

It's 3 a.m. January 1, 2021 12

Untitled..14

I Don't Know 15

Something Poetic 17

Pondering June..18

Drool.. 20

The Time to Look Back... 22

If It Were Only Me... 24

C 26

Dreams of Monday Morning 29

Around the Dinner Table..31

Staying Warm... 33

Time's Cruel Trick 34

Hold This... 35

Nose (or the unintended consequences of letting my
thoughts roll on) 37

The Spark in My Eye 40

Kookoo 41

The Girl I Prayed For.. 42

Cute but Naughty 44

The Girl I Think About When I Can't Sleep 45

Where's the One 47

To Fill a Void 49

At the Top I See Dragons 50

The Metaphor 52

Relieving Boredom 54

I Want 56

A poet's pick-up line in free form 60

Bugs 61

A New Place to Sit 63

Goddess 64

Writing 65

Obsessive Man Whore 67

A New Face in a New Place 69

The Wall of Ice 70

Great Debate 71

My Gamble 73

Just an Outside Perspective 75

For Those Far from Me 77

Dancer 78

How I Hope It Goes 80

Warden's Wishes 82

Oui 84

Untitled 85

I Want to Fall in Love 86

Ra 88

Long-Haired Rocker Boy 89

The Night Before the Day 91

On the Lake Fallen Log 93

Day Dreaming 95

The Broken Wrist Beauty 97

When the Sun Comes Up 98

Manic Depression 99

To Each Moment 100

A Toast for the Ice Queen 101

A Roast for the Ice Queen 103

Far Above 104
Ghost 105
T Talk 106
Belittled 108
Clogged Pipes 111
A Moth to a Flame 113
H 115
Aa 117
Addictions 119
To the Girl Who Complimented My Face 121
22 123
Most of the Time 125
Nightmare 127
For that Fairy 128
Flirty Poetry? 130
Stuff and Things 131
Changing Right 132
A Message for My Friend 134
It's Beautiful 135
Not Here 136
Not Doing Too Good 137
Brothers 138
Nonsense 139
Like a 140
A Poem in a Park 141
Close Walls 143
Battlefield 145
Thinkers 147
Stars 149
Savages 150
Kids with Phones 152
Something 154
Tomorrow Yesterday or in Between 157
A Shadow 159
Green-Haired Girl 161

Whoop-up Drive 163
The Old-School Fool 165
Sultry 167
What a Night 169
The Pigeon and the Duck 170
Don't Judge 171
Man of Thought 172
Want me? 174
Weathering Blue 175
Headlights 177
Walking in Old Shoes 178
Removing Negativity 179
Supposedly 181
Wicked Smile 183
Hold the Pose 185
At Every Turn 186
Falling Looks Graceful 187
Numbnessness 188
The Other Side of 4:00 AM 190
Growing Younger 193
Trade's Girl 194
What Are you Looking For? 195
Self-portrait in the style of Bukowski 197
The Boy with the Black Balloon 198
My Morbid Curiosity 200
The Wild Cat in a Box 202
Closing the Well 205
The Small-Town Registry Office 206
Don't Feel Like Satan 208
The McDonald's Playpen 210
Cold hands warm heart and the clock 214
Cold Hands Warm Heart 216
Embers 219
Septum 221
Shadow Boxed 223

The Broken Shuttered Window.. 226

Filling a day... 229

My First 231

The Mystic Mouse.. 233

Running in the hallway.. 235

Another Asshole's Apology.. 236

I Was Just A Crumb... 239

To Learn 242

Hey... 244

The Void Is Not a Void 245

One for My Mom.. 247

Everything Happens for a Reason... 248

The view from the mountain side 249

Untitled.. 250

Untitled.. 251

March 16, 2020.. 252

Bonjour

Hi. Thanks for picking this book up. If you promise not to put me down, I promise to give you some truths. My name is Kros, and I'm exactly like you. My atoms bounce like your atoms, you understand. I've lived a pretty regular life, perfectly unique. And like all life, filled with clichés. Filled in these pages are my little offerings; my thoughts transposed into a box, and then transferred to another box. I know I'm not right about everything, so I hope you find my subjective view of the chaos of life interesting. And I hope you know that by reading this, you've been a factor in making another human's life better. So I want to thank you. Thanks for reading my book. I sincerely hope I can, at the very least, alleviate some of the mundanity of life.

Au revoir.

It's Time (August 29, 2020)

It's time to put down the training wheels
Let's get this on track
It's time I cross these waters
And write something real

A script
A conversation
A book
A play
Just start small
And build it up
Layer by layer
Piece by piece
And don't be afraid
To just push it forward

Pipe and Typewriter

I'm in a house
Written about
By another poet

I'm sat
In front of a small desk
With a black and tarnished gold
Typewriter
It clicks and clacks
Just like you'd hope it would

In my mouth the pipe bobs
As I mindlessly whisper
The words I write
Pulling and pausing in thought

I stare wistfully
Onto the suburban street
A place
I've been before
And
Slept on the floor

A lady.
She comes from behind
Kisses my cheek
And leaves a cup of tea in my hand

There's a tremble

A cat sits in the sunlight
A yard to my right
And disappears

Another tremble
And dust falls from the ceiling
But there is no roof
No second floor

I put the tea down
I look away and type
I am handed another cup of tea
I put my hand in the tea

I piss my pants
I peal the skin from my face
I go to the door
And it's locked

I turn around
See the body of a comely lady
And out from the neck
A gnarled tendril of flesh rot

The pain in my chest is back
With every breath
I feel my stomach churn
And I hear a siren's song in my ear

I rush to my typewriter
And type while slime drools onto my shoulder

Don't get lost in the maze
Don't take pills without holding them in your hand
There's an evil in this land
A new kind of hell it will raise

We can speak and we can shout
But the loudest voices don't listen
To the brave we must instill doubt
And we must start over again

The fall of the Roman Empire
God will flood the Earth
And next time around
We'll take better care of our dirt

But these taps on the keys are my last
We sunk what we had too fast
It's a shame to know that
I'll blink and not see the blast

LET ME TELL YOU ABOUT THIS JOURNEY I'M ON

A long time ago in a town far a way
There was a dad yelling at his son
It's a memory that would change the course
Of both of their lives

That boy was passed on a deep sense of low self-worth
As is family tradition
And that boy decided
He'd do everything he could to prove himself

The obstacles in front of him were no different than they were
for anybody else
But his goals became unattainably high
He began to dream of towers in his name
And an endless fulfillment of love and lust

And he carries that weight wherever he goes
Knowing he could be doing more
Knowing he could be fighting harder
Knowing he probably won't succeed

This seed of selfish doubt planted in him
Grows fruits of motivation and poison
And they corrupt
His perception of the world

And so the boy does what he can
To find out what it means to be a man
He's searching for love
And he can't stop trying for the top

Will he ever find what he's looking for

A's Ask

I'll tell you in a diddle
That it's surprisingly little
That someone reach out
For the words I tout

It puts a smile on my face
For it's the challenge I chase

Writing words for women who will woah
In essence

You've motivated me
To write for your beauty
And for that I thank you
The practice will always make do

I like the smile
Gandalf
And I like the bangs
Top shelf
I like the piercings
Double nose
I think I'd like a lot about you
But who knows
'as A's ask been answered?
A promise of poem and prose

An Empty Night

Thankfully it's warmer now
I find myself strolling through the dark most nights
It's
Nice

The stars are brightest
In the park where I'm paranoid
I always feel on edge
Though I know there's no real chance of danger
The rattlesnakes are asleep
I think
And this neighbourhood is too rich from oil
And too new
No one in this area has been rejected by society
Yet

The two issues on my mind tonight
One as old as my ambitions:
How am I going to be successful
And one as old as my anxiety:
Why do I have a hard time being myself

And I guess that begs the question
What even am I

I don't think anything will be resolved tonight
The matters of my day to day

While still happening day to day
Will have to be resolved day to day
I just can't help but feel the same depression over the fact
that my life isn't some endless hedonistic bliss.

Food and women
Fun and excitement
Empathy and connection
Even if I get these things
I just want more

I still have time
But if I want to really fulfill my desires
I'll have to give more
More effort
More passion
But of course
These are always my thoughts
On nights as empty as this

Love Like Shakespeare

The man in the middle of history
That's at the start of all written arts

Separated by disease not dynasty
What the future holds is a mystery

I'm sure we'll fare better than the two
Who were just fucking ready to die

My prose or word may not be masterful
But'iambic pentameter I can pull

However I'm not sure I can make it
The meter asks me to do oh so much

So to put it all in one last couplet
I will say this to the gorgeous ginger

No sweat no fret we will meet again soon
For we have yet to see spring's fated swoon

It's 3 a.m. January 1, 2021

I am getting high
I'm looking at the sky
And I've just seen a shooting star
Foretelling a good year

I'm back in bed now
For the past week or so I've been feeling
A coming change
I've started to reach the end course
Of a two-year stoner bachelor's degree
Done by year three

. . . My dog's with me now
My pretty girl
My good ol' doggo
My stubborn pathfinding companion
You know a dog really forces you to maintain a lifestyle
Or live in guilt for staying stubborn

She's annoyed I'm not giving her attention
So I tell her that when inspiration hits I gotta catch it
I have no clue what I'm writing half the time
I don't think it's great half the time
But when my heart and soul start pumping words
I just got to take them down
Otherwise
They're gone

Anyways . . .

A star falls
And I see the stellar darting trail,
An arc of magic,
A lucky sign

Perhaps it's not my place to take meaning in
Meaningless Astronomical Affects
But my god, man
What are the odds
I almost doubt my eyes
But I know what I saw
There was a meteor in those skies

And seeing something like that
Really fires me up

But
I've finally realized
The hours are nearing a summer's dawn
And though this night may last long
I have to try and catch the faint day
So I beg sleep
Take me away

UNTITLED

Look inward
Be who you want to be
Decide what's best for you
You have the power to do the right thing

I Don't Know

I write
There's a chance you do too
Now I don't know you
And I bet you don't know me

My words
You see a collection of
Garbled thoughts
Misled mis-intentions

I'm some kind of fucked-up fighter
In a tight kind of shell
A tough cut of meat
Behind a soft boy vibe

I don't know

I'm twenty-two right?
It should be my catchphrase

Keep context in mind is all I'm saying

SOMETHING POETIC

Through twice-lived eyes
And windowed skies
I've come to realize
We all surround ourselves in lies

If honesty is the complete
Full communication
Of all information
Then we all stand with dishonest feet

Dishonesty can be dangerous
You need a little trust
Or it could happen to be
You'll lose a kidney

So if you'd like to take that risk
Of utmost honesty
To be completely free
You just got to ask

Goodnight to those that can live their own virtues
Tonight I pray to the sandman

Pondering June

In the rain
By the corner
With all the spider webs
A young
Dumb duck
Considers his sexuality

A chorus of
Patter patter patter patter
Endless
Continuous
Rhythmic
Patter

Splashing on glass tabletops
Covered in dirt
And clay

A wet dog bone on the carpet
Surrounded by the seeds of trees
A black and silver metal
Barbeque

Where does love live
Where does it go
Does love come to you?

Once I find a home

I will be free to find
A partner in soul and mind

DROOL

I am a complex machine
Of a million billion tiny robots
With a history of action forever written in stone
That nobody knows
And a future with an unlimited amount of
possibilities
That nobody knows

I transform the dead into energy
I observe a universe of interaction
Mortality stands on my shoulder
I've felt love
And certainly sorrow
I've seen birth
And a corpse on his deathbed

Birds with stiff wings have carried me
Cars on boats have sailed me
Trains through the city have railed me
Dogs have asked me for a bone
Wild cats have cuddled in my arms
I've stepped underneath great trees
The river flow has picked fights with me

Hawks have hunted
Cats who killed

Mice that snack
On me

The wind has tried to knock me off the back
Of my blue sparrow
That carries me on winding paths
On cliffsides

In galleries I've seen through the eyes
Of a thousand artists
In books I've read the minds
Of a thousand writers
In albums I've heard the words
Of people with something to say

I stepped on the mousetrap
Twice
And danced in the halls with the dancer
Who can't be called cute

I accept that I can't cut off my tail

Yet here I am
Sitting around
Making drool

THE TIME TO LOOK BACK

December 26,
2020
What a year
Another step
Toward a bleak future

If life was one big marathon
I spent this year
Sitting and having a slice
Of pizza while catching my breath

Not too long
Till the coals are set beneath me
And I walk paths
Others would avoid

I just need to make that choice
And take a deep breath

Or maybe just close my eyes
And walk with the wind

Rivers and currents
Wind and clouds
The metaphors are there
But the reality is it's not that easy

If only I could just walk across
A bridge of burning charcoal
But you know what I got to do?
'Cause I don't
There is no stream to follow
I'm on my own path
And I see casualties of false futures
And I know I have a lot of pitfalls I need to avoid

My mistakes this year are falling behind the wayside of my mind
Though the emotions trail close behind
I had a low year
Like lots have
And while the highlights weren't exposé worthy
They sprinkled joy on the shit cake
Of the year of our Lord
Two thousand and twenty

What nonsense will this decade continue to bring
And will this year be better than the last

If It Were Only Me

Surrounded by seas
Of dead fallen leaves

If it were only me
Left
After a worldwide death
I'd be a little glad
I'd wander the streets and paths
I'd think it's not so bad
To have a world to myself
An endless cavern
Of human invention
To delve deep
And discover its secrets

If it were only me
Left
After a global pandemic
I'd be a little sad
I'd miss my mom
And the repercussions of laziness
To be in the world alone
With no one to share in the wonder
No one but me
To see the pistol I put to my head
And no one
To clean up the mess

Two dozen
Maybe two hundred
Or even two thousand
Hell
Two million
Anything other than
Seven billion
The drains clogged
With ripped-out hair
And the blood
Is overflowing
We
Need less of we
There's no point in covering the globe
In thirsty humans
If they're all just going to divide themselves
And then get into a fucking pissing contest
Of who can produce
And consume
More

But maybe the point of life isn't to live
Maybe the point is to light the biggest fire
Before you die
I know there's no point
There's just what we do
What we hide
And what we justify

If it were only me
Making the decisions
I'd try to do something smarter
But with seven billion shouts
The best I could ever hope for
Is to die
A quiet martyr

C

I don't think
I could ever find the words
To do justice
For what I want to say about you

I've written a lot of pretty poems
For a lot of pretty girls
But all of them added together
Wouldn't be enough

A love poem
Something special
For someone special
And I'm writing one

For someone I haven't met yet

I know you're shy
Seeing you makes me fly
It feels like you've lit an ember in me
One that makes me want to live passionately

Could it be
After so long
So much pain
So much heartache
I've found someone to
End my lost wandering

I'd cross a thousand miles
To see you smile
I'll spend all my years
Wiping away any of your tears

And protecting you from any fears

I worry I come on too strong
So I won't make this too long
But I feel this night I met you, C,
Was the day I felt most happy

And put all my heart
Into this small piece of art
The Best Years of My Life

I spend a lot of time
Yearning for better years
For timeless memories
Total satisfaction

I know that can't really exist
It's human nature to thirst

But from where I am right now
I feel pretty close

When I'm by your side
When I'm on your screen
When I'm in your ears
And invading your daydreams

I feel
A lot really
But what I feel most
Is cared for

A caring I've been looking for
A place where the time before
And after
Still feel good
Just because I get to hold you in my mind
And never feel scared

My goodness do I feel safe
In this turbulent world
I hold the stalwart sensation
That is my beautiful C

Dreams of Monday Morning

Last night
I dreamed
A world of anxiety
The details lost
But the emotions stayed
Into the waking world

As I turned over
To check the time on my phone
I saw exactly what I wanted to see
A message to make me happy

Smiling I sent a response set a timer
And let the soft blankets work their magic

When the timer ran out
I still had not gotten my fill
And through the magic of the internet
I decided not to leave my bed yet

Now me and my girl
In our beds twirl
And dream of the Monday mornings

Where we don't have to leave the bed
And can just stare at each other instead
In bliss
And coziness

AROUND THE DINNER TABLE

A family
And flocks
Find a
Fill and

More

Groups of two
The mothers' duo
And trio
Of couples

Bread broken
Politics spoken
Stories of
Falling down

On Sunday
The love falls on family
What's more spiritual
Than being with shared blood

This knotty-haired sewer rat
Was kindly welcomed
To a warm meal
And a series of hidden compliments

Truly kind

Staying Warm

It's getting cold
And soon
The white snow
Will cover the ground
And the harsh winds
Will throw it in your face
And the short days
Will mangle the mind
But
I have an angel by my side this time
A sweet and shy
Girl that makes me cry
At her pure
Soft
Beauty
Someone who can
Keep me warm when it's cold
And
Show me the light when it's dark

Let us avast ourselves of the cruel Jack Frost and find
ourselves fleet-footed fleeing to the warm safety of blankets
and bosoms. Let us stay up through the night in good spirits
with silly antics and sexual pleasures. Let loneliness fall
wayside, and let coziness reside. The cold season's coming,
C, and I'm glad I've found you at last. I think this might be my
favourite winter season yet.

TIME'S CRUEL TRICK

Why is it so
That every second
I'm away from you
Feels like sludge
Time crawling through mud
A limbo
Of responsibility and work

But

When I'm with you
There's never enough time
Hours of smiles and laughter
Gone in minutes
The eternity I could spend looking into those
Beautiful blue eyes
Gone in a moment

Sitting by a clock ticking
Thinking of us fricking
Longing for my belonging
Cuddled up in your warmth

If I could
I'd put a stop to all of time
And stay in a moment
Right after I made you smile

Hold This

Hold this for me, will you, darling
Careful, it's a bit heavy
And cold
And don't mind it's endless
Droning beat
It just kind of does that

Hold this for me please
And try not to drop it
There's not a lot of people
I'd trust to have this
Doing that has left me
To pick up a lot of broken pieces

Hold this for me
Because I think you have the key
That'll crack this iron lockbox
And let the ol' timepiece
Finally get a breath
Of fresh air
That smells like bubble gum

Hold this for me
It's my heart, C,
I want you to have it
Because I think only you
Who's so kind

And so sweet
Should hold on to something
So close to me

Hold this heart
Feel its beat
Let me lie on your chest
And finally understand rest
I promise I will do my part
If you can just
Hold this heart

Nose (or the unintended consequences of letting my thoughts roll on)

Honestly
Living blows
I capture that often
In prose
After all my living
This I knows
Life is just a series
Of stubbed toes
But if there's one thing
I suppose
That'll keep me smiling
Is your cute nose

You know the nose is the second body part
Most broken just before the heart

But I suppose there's no point worrying
At some point they all stop beating

The world is dying
And fools are lying
Here I am trying
To say the most in writing

But my heart beats too blue
I don't know the meaning of true
And I'm drowning in the sea
Of everything expected of me

Float or suffocate
Plan before it's too late
I don't want to end up in some job
Serving the worst of the mob

You know as a species
We've cut billions of trees
But here I am under one
Sitting in the sun

I had hope here that I'd find
Some words for a girl to occupy the mind
But as usual in my journey to create
Happiness, I've fallen to a different fate

Doom
Gloom
And the feeling
That there's no such thing as fun

I hope the first part made you smile
I think I must have eaten something vile
That's upsetting my stomach bile
And darkened the theme for a while
Made me add on a sadness pile

It helps when I think of your eyes
Or laying my head on your thighs
Everything from your head to toes
Especially your wonderful nose

I think I should stop before
The stomach bug
Pulls the rug
And knocks me back to the floor

THE SPARK IN MY EYE

Every genuine warm smile
Every cuddling shift
Every pretty word I write
Is for you
Spark in my eye

Every opportunity to watch you
When your back's turned
Or your gaze
Is cast elsewhere
I ogle my eyes
On a beauty that beholds

Hotter
Than a burning star
More
Sexy and soft
Than red velvet
And a good woman too

So here's to you
Oh spark of my eye
Here's to the days and nights
That are brighter
When I'm by your side

KOOKOO

A couple of crazy kookoo cats
Cuddling in each other's laps
Craving endless naps
A lucky bunch of saps
One with beautiful baps
The other gifted with raps
Found each other with the help of apps
Now each other's favourite contacts

THE GIRL I PRAYED FOR

I think back
To a rainy day in July
I was outside
Thinking about my life gone by
And my life going forward
The pitter-patter
Helps me know
That you can only go so low
I knew hard times were coming
I knew I was going to need something
To help me get through
The slew.

So I prayed
I'm not a man of prayer
When I was a kid I prayed to die
And when the morning passed me by
And I was still alive
I knew me and God wouldn't always jive

But this time on a hope and a prayer
To make the balance fair
I was sent a beautiful angel

Life sure is a lot easier with her by my side
Someone with whom I can confide

Who keeps me in my stride
And will one day join me on a carousel ride

Non adieu today
For I want you to stay
Let's continue spending the day
Enjoying life's play

CUTE BUT NAUGHTY

The girl
Inspires all sorts of
Angelic
And
Devilish
Thoughts

Cuddles
And
Wholesome care
A collection of kitties
And a mountain of softness
Cute dates
Shy smiles
A good girl
To warm my heart

Moans
And
A lewd attraction
To a soft body
With all sorts of fun parts
To play with
Big and round and juicy
A good girl
To satisfy my lust

THE GIRL I THINK ABOUT WHEN I CAN'T SLEEP

I don't know if it's me missing her marvellous curves
Or hearing her comforting words
Or the way she looks at me with her innocent eyes
Or the way she warms my hand with her thighs
But it's hard to get her out of my mind
Especially when it comes to sleep time
The dreams had while still awake
When you think of the twists and turns of fate
I think about her and I miss the warmth
The hold she has on my heart

I think of our first date a lot
The crunch of autumn
Her beautiful blue eyes against a backdrop of brown leaves
and trees

But mostly I think of the softness
Of her caress
The gentle touch of an angel
And the weird noises we make at each other
Those are always great
Where words fail me
A bark grunt pop or *awoo*
Helps me feel like I'm not alone
If there's one thing that helps me sleep

More than anything else
It's when she shares my bed
And I know she slumbers softly
My bed would feel cozier than ever
But sadly
Right now
She's not beside me
And so I'm left with just the memory
Of what it feels like
To sleep softly

WHERE'S THE ONE

Where's the one
That'll smoke a joint with me on my way home from the
mountain
Go for a walk
And just silently enjoy
The serenity

Where's the one
That'll cuddle on the couch with me
While sheepdogs sing
And the evening's entertainment
Are four hands searching for sweet spots

Where's the one
That'll compete with me
Over the stupidest silliest games
Respecting each other's wins and losses
And always cheering each other on

Where's the one
Who's happy
To just
Look
Into my eyes
While I look at them

Where's the one
Who'll share a dance
With the kid
That dances alone

Where's the one
Who thinks I'm fun
Who thinks I'm hot
Who thinks I'm where it's at

Where's the one
That won't sleep around
That I can trust
And call
When the cold months
Get too dark

Where's the one
That sees depth
In the shallow
And knows how sweet
Eye candy can be

Where's the one
That doesn't snort dust
Or roll in cat shit
That can crack a joke
That's actually funny

I hope
If I grow
And be my best me
The one
Will come
And I won't ruin it

To Fill a Void

To fill the void you'll need more than

The light from the sun rise
The glow from a full moon
The miracle of life
Or the mystery of death

To fill the void you need what can't be found
You need to turn around
You need to let go
And the void has to fall behind

Nothing to rid nothing
Because everything can't fill the endless

AT THE TOP I SEE DRAGONS

Can you see them
On top
Of those
Unbelievably high
Towers of gold

In some sort of
Manic
Sociopathic
Competition
To stack the tallest
Collection of coins

The dragons smile
But they do not see

Their towers
Balance on the backs
Of the weak
Misfortunate
And dead

Can you feel their wingbeats
Can you see
Their blurry shadows
Know that their hoards
Can't stand against the strength

Of the hundreds of thousands
And millions and billions
That will one day
Look up
And
Tear down

You know now more than ever
I hear the ticktock
For those
At the
Tip
Top

THE METAPHOR

Who's gonna stand by my side
And live their life with me
When mine
Is just looking for metaphors

Oh, there's silly ones
That trash
Yeah?
That's me

There's cute ones
You
Me?
Are a mouse

There's mean ones
And there's green ones
There's lean ones
And don't forget
The sheen ones

It's like a
No

It's a mad world
With loose children
And rampant rats

A fight for
Cupid's bow
And a clash between
Piano and choir
Accompany thee
Daughters of daughters
Sons of sons
Let the cross
Balance on water
And watch the world shake
To a more rhythmic beat

Let the empires know
This king
Will usurp
The crown

RELIEVING BOREDOM

Monkey brains with dopamine machines
Endless scrolling and endless content
Doesn't matter if you're
Heartbroken or homeless
The hours march on
And the days waste away

Substance
Grown, manufactured, or otherwise
It's what we all crave
That meaning of being

Real and raw
What makes us human
An unrequited desire
To not do nothing

And instead do something
Or do someone
Like biological lobotomites
Slaves to desire

A metaphorical mal-harmony
The thirsty slurp to salivate
A degenerate dive
To take what you can from someone else

But you can't always get what you want
Cried the cynic
Furiously masturbating
To pictures of grass

All's I know is that
Like all the rest
I want
How much I'll never know

I WANT

I am still filled with dreams
I have things I want to do in my life

I want to capture beauty in as many photos as I can
I want to see the world
I want to find healthy love
I want a good career

I want to master control of my body
I want to master the mysteries of words
I want to serenade a pretty lady
I want someone to make something for me

I want to soar in the skies in every way
I want to explore a Shinto temple
I want to walk on bridges of glass
I want to sit on a train in the sky

I want to journey from France to Berlin
From Tokyo to Kyoto
From Lisbon to Barcelona
From London to Edinburgh
From Seattle to LA
From Boston to New York
From Ontario to Montreal
From Amsterdam to Copenhagen

I want to see the history of Italy
I want to see the cherry blossoms in Japan
I want to see the spirit of America
I want to see the battlefield of a generation

I want to skate in the walking paths of a million towns
I want to make a movie
I want to see the graves of the brave
I want to be a leader of people

I want to be part of the generation that survives
The earth's greatest battles
I want to see the world grow young
As I grow old

I want to be rich and
I want to reduce poverty
I want my name to mean something
I want my spotlight to be good

I want to drive a motorcycle
I want to smoke weed and cuddle
I want to look in a mirror and feel proud
I want to wear cool clothes

I want to see my kid grow up
I want to see a human become in front of me
I want to know what they want from life
I want to watch them learn to see

I want to see creativity
I want to watch the artist
I want to have a dancing partner
I want to have a sparring partner

I want to be confident
I want to be beautiful
I want to make people laugh
I want to feel smart

I want to see cool buildings
I want to stand on rooftops
I want to make a mark on history
I want to watch humanity step into the stars

I want to see an alien
I want magic to be real
I want to make games
I want to be part of a team

I want to solve puzzles
I want to self-discover
I want to predict people
I want to be wise

I want to sing a song that tells a story
I want to experience curveballs
I want to have a mentor
I want to mentor someone

I want to have my own steam room
I want a super computer
I want a nice chair and
I want a nice desk
I want a smart home
I want a personal chef
I want a personal trainer and
I want a personal assistant

I want a team of R&D

I want a foot in the space race
I want to experience extravagance
I want to live in a city apartment

I want to take so many trains
I want to fly in planes
I want to wander in museums
I want to explore galleries

I want to go to concerts
I want to hit the open road
I want to speak the truth
I want to live honestly

I want to lie
I want to be a character
I want to perform
I want to be on stage

I want to be in a movie
I want to be able to go anywhere
I want to make money
I want to sharpen my mind

I want to golf with businesspeople
I want to go to the bar after work with the team
I want to go to a friend's wedding
I want to play sports

Nothing is holding me back
I just have to do
And I know I can
I feel like the road in front of me is one I want to travel

That's a very good feeling

A POET'S PICK-UP LINE
IN FREE FORM

Honesty
Best policy
So here I go
Kelly
I say to thee
Like a puppy
I want to hold you in my arms
But I'm a dumb slut
And I can't put up
With the steps between screen and
Swooning
But I know a thing or two
About the labia vulva and clit too
So if you want to feel
These magic hands
From this magic man
Then let's make a plan
Otherwise
I'm sure you'll do fine without this dean's list dingus

BUGS

It bugs me how
You said something
And my worldview shifted
And
It bugged me
How it never felt like
You were talking to me
Distance
From beside each other
And
It bugged
Me
How
You never could follow through
On anything
Work
School
Life
Love
You teased everyone
And
Yourself

You can be indecisive but still follow through

It bugged me
How I

Needed you to see everything
I think
In an effort
To be less boring
I threw a million lines
Into barren seas
I need time to get comfortable
With
Some
One
And
I always saw our hourglass near empty

It bugs me how
I still write about you
But it's for me

But

The only other thing to talk about
Today
Is the mosquitoes

A New Place to Sit

A new place to sit
Is all I need

If I could sum up
Every time in my life
I've consistently found bliss
Is when I find

A new place to sit
A new view to see
From a new place it
Is all a gallery

GODDESS

It's a good word
A lot of meaning
Power beauty and grace all in one
Sending heathens and heretics on the run

Though I don't know you
I think it's a wonderful mark
The Queen of the dark
I'm sure it's true

If I could bow before the goddess
And give one thoughtful prayer
I'd ask for holistic hedonism;
To rule the world

Or
To know
If the joy you got from matching with me
Matched the joy I felt matching with you

This weird little app truly is a dopamine machine

WRITING

It really befuddles me
To think about
The idea that no thoughts are new

Fuck specifics
Or how things tie together
Those emotions
Those thoughts
Those behaviours
Have been felt by another

And so when it comes to writing
How could I not feel a fraud
After all everything I've written
Must have been thought by someone else
Or worse we've written entwined words in different books

Something to ponder
On a depressing night
Preceded by a depressing day
Wicked by an intimate morning

It's going to be a long night.

I'm beholden to wicked thoughts
Saddening memories
And scaring soothes

I'm frightened by the demands of the formal word
And I question its merit
It seems so inefficient
I can write all these thoughts and facts
Or I could succinctly transfer knowledge
But I can't do both

If I were in charge
I'd understand
There's power in people
Always be critical
But let others think
What they think

. . . Now get that to print

OBSESSIVE MAN WHORE

I dream almost every night
While lying listlessly awake
Of a dozen different lives
With a dozen different women

I dream of ambition
Us together in the spotlight
Dynamos of our fields
Respected by our peers
To the world we are invincible
And to each other we are vulnerable
In the differences between night and day
Our weaknesses covered by strengths overlay

I dream of coziness
Us looking in the endless skies
Of one another's eyes
The days come and go
Balanced and wholesome
A familial life
Kids grandkids in-laws and extended
There's a real sense of belonging
One I've never felt

I dream of adventure
Expanded horizons of life and lust
Tasting new fruits of flesh

And pleasing virgins
A creature of desire
With tongues never tired
To be wanted
To be needed
To be devoured

I dream of someone
Who is everyone
Endless givers to selflessly stand above me
So I can endlessly drink their blood
'Cause if my mouth were to dry for just a second
I'd start crying like the babe ripped from the teat

A New Face in a New Place

I can only imagine the numbers
In this age of apps
You go somewhere new
And thousands of masks wait staring at you
It can be unnerving
And unsettling
'Cause every mask hides deeper desires

But boundless boons of ego-raising loons can be found,
As well as simple soul suckers as far as the eyes can see

'Course the only real way to start lifting masks
Takes time, effort, and questions asked
A tedious process
That can leave a mess

THE WALL OF ICE

It's
Hard
To turn a stranger into something more

We all have a natural
Insulated wall of ice
That keeps us safe from being burned

Some break the ice
Some wait for it to melt
And others can't get through

That's kinda how it feels from me to you

But I'll bide my time
While the thoughts of me in your head
Might end up entirely dead

I'd rather that
Than trying to break the ice
And fucking up something fragile

I just can't help but stare at that wall

GREAT DEBATE

An exchange
Pros cons
Thought opinions
Back and forth

A good exercise
Train the brain
Learn about
Precision and research

A battle
Mine yours
Trivial matters
Spit and spat

The Devil's advocate
What's really true
What is there to learn
What could be moral

For some
A test
A demonstration of wisdom
And wit

Anyways
What if humans are the virus
For planets
And Covid is the vaccine?

My Gamble

Forgive me I tend to ramble
But here I lay my given gamble

I bet
Talking with you would be fun
I bet
Together far we could run
I bet
That though we haven't met
That maybe you could be the one

Romantic or creepy
Your interpretation isn't up to me
But stick with me and you'll see
What luck fate can be

I want to talk about the nuances of life
I want us to share a joint at night
I want two halves to make a half dead whole

I
Am attracted to you
A fool who follows rules
Just fucking slobbering drool

From a few words I sense you're tired of a world looking down
on you

I can imagine that's tough
So I'll say without extra fluff

That I hope to be your equal

A gamble it's my greed
But I can't explain why it's me you need

It's insecurity you see
The poison trapped in me
I feel if I don't wow you now
The play will be over before the bow

And it's a risky play
The philosopher finding a debate
And the fool finding far-flung fate
But who knows what's brought with May

My gamble
Some words on a screen
Were they written right or wrong
The odds of finding the one are long
And I've probably come on too strong
But I honestly just want to talk more and see if we get along

What do you say
Gorgeous goth girl R?

JUST AN OUTSIDE PERSPECTIVE

I can only imagine
What it's like
To be orbited
To be followed
To be begged
To be given
And to be expected

I can only imagine
It alters you
How you see people
How you interact with strangers
How you decide what's moral
How you express yourself

The guilt
That's built
By thousands of
Selfish givers
It must grow stale

Fear replaces fun
And defence mechanisms
Keep you safe

And the blind
Seethe from far away

Another life altered by the box
It happens to even the smartest fox

Something something
We live in a society
Something something
Making your own destiny
Something something
Sex appeal
Shot in the foot

For Those Far from Me

Tinder
'Tis a silly place

I've been home a couple days
Though I'm glad it's no longer my home
It's a mess
Believe me

And during my stay
I've matched with many
Pretty, interesting, cool people
But you all seem so far away

So I just want to say
To those far away from me
You are all fucking awesome
Though we may never meet
This may be our only greet
You're all really heckin' neat
You keep doing you
Find the meaning of true

Anyways goodbye to all of you
I didn't get a chance to say hi to

DANCER

I don't know much about you
Just some picture clues
But you sure make a cool elf
You know how to take care of yourself

As songs can set moods
I'm sure she's got moves
If I could offer any assurance
I'd say you can do you

This one's for the dancer
V

Your beauty beams
And sex appeal gleams
You've got it from head to feet
Your elegance I declare elite
Your self-awareness I think is neat
And we might not get the chance to meet
But none of my plans ever end up concrete
And with that this rhyme is complete

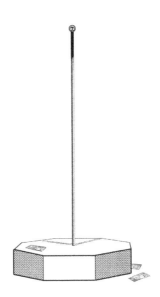

How I Hope It Goes

It's Friday
six or seven
I pick you up
Opening the door
'Cause I'm a gentleman

Bad Company's self-titled album is playing
I'm hoping my sunglasses look cool in the orange
While we talk about
What we like
And what we're like

It's always awkward meeting app acquaintances
But the music musings are shared
We're on a roll with the rock paired
After burning some gas and driving the scenic pass
I'll ask you over for weed and pizza

We'll share a smoke with the setting sun
Eat some slices to a movie dumb and fun
We'll slip into a cuddle puddle
And if the moment feels right
I'll make my move
To honk
Ra's boob

Perhaps it's not wise to predict in prose
Or hope for how a date goes
Spontaneity may not suit me
But I say in all honesty
I just hope to make you smile

WARDEN'S WISHES

Crouching beneath the stars
In my concrete prison
I hear the guard walking by
Twenty past midnight

I fixate
On my breath
And my words

I stand

"There's a time I'm missing"
Behind these miserable bars
I'm destined for the stars
He said as blind as a bat

Just some kinda
Stupid self-belief

He
. . .
Felt an anxious rush

Dilated depression
Just kicks in

"March, May, whenever comes the opportunity"
He makes an attack
To cut the slack
And catch a shooting star

OUI

I'll gaslight
Say all sorts of sweets
For the chance to see teats
You're right

I spent twenty years a kissless loner
Went to college became a stoner
Made my way into some panties
And ever since then became a filler of fantasies

Zeina, I'll have you know
Whatever you think of this hoe
I'm just a depressed joker
Who enjoys playing people poker

So comrade of ironic fad
I'd certainly be more than glad
To scribble some stupid words
As tone-deaf as sea birds

UNTITLED

Warmth
That's what I mostly remember
From the lake
A warmth
Like piss running down the leg
Of my heart
It's really quite nice
Shame about the stain though

I Want to Fall in Love

Love
Not lust
Not desire
Not infatuation
Not contentment
Not anything but
Pure
Complete
Unconditional
Love

I want someone by my side at my best
I want someone by my side at my worst
I want to look into their eyes and feel bliss
I want them to occupy my mind completely

Together
Wonder bound
Through tales trials and toasts
Complete like heavenly bodies in orbit

Love
Lucid and real
Love
Strong like apes together

Love
The luxury of life
Given to those willing to work

I'll try my best

RA

I suppose if I ever wrote a song I'd have to find another name

A smile as pretty as your anthem
A girl who's seen the world and then some
Let's try and vibe tonight if you're free
I'll show you exactly my quality

I'm not a man of money
Only sometimes am I funny
I can rock your world with just my hands
And I've sadly not travelled many lands
I'll answer anything honestly
As long as you can promise me
That you'll try to do the same
Not lost in life's little game

I must admit it's hard to write
For in my mind there's a fight
Between the artist looking for "it"
And the guy just trying to touch a tit

So, Ra,
For as little as I've known ya
I must ask of thee
What do you want
With me

And maybe we can go from there

Long-Haired Rocker Boy

Take me back to
Rock'n'Roll High School
And play me that
Old Time Rock & Roll

Little old to be called a
Teenage Dirtbag
But I'm still
Feeling Good

Sometimes I get those
Roadhouse Blues
But I'm still high and dry
No Rain

I ain't looking to be no
Heartbreaker
Just a vibing
Voodoo Child

So will we go
Where Eagles Dare
'Cause these days I
Don't Fear The Reaper

On the hunt for
Sweet Emotion

Not trying to put anyone
Under My Thumb

So, T,
Let's put on a
Rock & Roll Band
Hit the road and
Run to the Hills

THE NIGHT BEFORE THE DAY

I wonder how long it'll take
To drain that well
Of literary tell

The night before the Day

Tomorrow I am me
And tomorrow you are you
And as a pair of two
We'll probably vibe awkwardly

But once that threshold's broken
The conversation starts flowin'

And then there's the park
And then there's the wind
And then there's these two
Giggling goblins
Laughing at something
Incredibly dumb
And the hearts start to drum

And I'm pretty sure I'm writing a wack early 2000s pop-punk song

I should probably stop trying to foretell
And try to relax for a spell

Tomorrow is going to be

Tomorrow I'm going to try my best

On the Lake Fallen Log

That
Beautiful
Sun-cast shade of orange
Bouncing in the blowing breeze

Falling on her
Great green garment

It really is a savoury sight
And I can only reckon it might
Stay in my mind's eye a while
For whenever I need a smile

There she is standing tall
And me in awe of it all
A scene of serenity
Something not always found easily

On the dead walk those alive
It's on juxtaposition we thrive
For every part in the art
There's a mart and a chart

A people person
And a money man
An authentic actress
And an academic

An animator
And a gamer
Loud
And listless

Both with words worth writing

Some
Are superstitious about a ginger stealing souls
Well some
Are salacious stoners smoking rolls

Like some kind of story for the stars behind that deep blue sky
Starting on that lake fallen log

DAY DREAMING

Still can't get over how awesome of a name Day is

In the quiet moments
In the warm shower
Out on a sunny road
And right before bed

I wonder about this
I'd love to talk more about that
I shoulda kept that conversation going
'Cause I'm curious to know more

She's been renting space in my mind
And it's a very bright corner

It feels like a guilty pleasure
Thinking about her

It makes me want to do better
I want to impress her

I want her
To stick around
It's really not that profound

I've just been lost Day dreaming

But I'm anxious
I want to see more of her
And of course
I want to see more of her

But I'm scared
Just so goddamned scared
You know how much it hurts
Being vulnerable
And exposed
Again and again
With relentless rejecters

Like some kind of addict
To heartaches and headaches
I'm covered in invisible bruises
And old
Old scars

I want to chase what could be
I don't want to settle for what's meant to be
I forge my own path of destiny
And I have Day dreams that I want to make reality

I feel the familiar curse
Of a fucked-up childhood
Continue to cloud my mind

THE BROKEN WRIST BEAUTY

What a woman
The kind with spirit
And whimsy

I get the feeling that hanging with you
We'd find some way to
Fly to the moon

I must refrain
From spilling to much
Admiration

I hope the docs give you something good
Long gone the days of setting bones to wood
I'd kiss it better if I could

Anyhow
I don't really have much to say
But here's to a speedy recovery

And to a future date with the delightful Day

WHEN THE SUN COMES UP

Cops and crimes
Fools with rhymes
A raccoon scrounges in the trash
Kurclunk boom bash

Banana on head he leans on the edge
He wants to be done with the sludge
That sticks to his fur
He wants it for her

The girl with the pleasance of the afternoon sun
Captured in her hair
The smiling star
The fair-skinned fun supplier
The one with the pics of
Loops smoking loops blowing loops
The gamer girl
Production pro
Badass motherfucker

The first rays of sun beam over the horizon
Softly

MANIC DEPRESSION

When I'm alone I want to be with people
When I'm with people I want to be alone

All anticipation turns to ash
And smiles mask sadness

In my head are endless images
Of me bleeding profusely

It feels like everyone is lying to me
And everything good is evil

I can't cry or get excited
My heart feels like stone

I am waste
Littered in a place
That no one's going to clean up

To Each Moment

A memory
Lost in itself
Each moment
Trying to savour
What might not last
Was it me
Who knows
I had fun
But
Was I there
Still
A memory
To each moment

A Toast for the Ice Queen

There's depth
In those eyes
I'm sure they tell no lies

A troubled past
Won't leave us fast
But you look like someone who can survive a long haul

Short cute and sexy
With wicked wavy hair
Forgive my urge to stare

I'm probably not hood enough for you
So I want to say this true
I'm sure you'll do great whatever you do

But in my mind I see
A portrait of you and me

Sat next to a window on a rainy day
And the silence is so softly disrupted by the pitter-patter
I couldn't imagine anything better
Maybe the dice will roll that way

Anyways here's to you, J,
The hippie with the nose ring
Who makes my heart sing
A one in a million

A Roast for the Ice Queen

I can only imagine you have more
Dissociative defence mechanisms
Than an American government organization

You look like you give
The sloppiest sluttiest head
Because you like to blow your problems away

Do all the necklaces you adorn
Try to distract the forlorn
Death in your eyes

I bet you're just like me
A slothful carcass who feels sadness
Is the only real catharsis

A li'l hippie a li'l hood
Someone who's there when the vibe is good
And never sticks around to clean up the mess

FAR ABOVE

How far above is she
What do they see
What's in his dreams

What gets done and why
Fuck no that's beside the point

What I wanna know
Is if there was a ladder
Where would I be

It's a dumb question
Filled with bad patterns
Call it the cat killing curiosity

Ghost

All alone
Half past one
In the morning
On a Thursday

Or I guess Friday

I wish I was haunted
By a well-meaning spirit
That'd stay up with me
Burn the midnight oil

Or I guess I just want a companion

T Talk

What's there?
On the other side
Of this
Godforsaken app

Art
Do you make things?
Or just like looking?
What way do you see the world?

Writer
God, I'm curious
What words do you use?
Maybe we could share a muse

Museum
People are strange
And they like to put things in big rooms
Could we wander together through big rooms filled with facts?

Coffee
I like tea
But it's never the beverage
It's the atmospheres and addictions

Trivia
What is a nice night in?
Watching *Jeopardy*
Here's the clue

BELITTLED

The sadness
And self-esteem issues
That choke me
Are fucking lame
To put it bluntly

Jealousy
Especially when it's hypocritical
Is my darkest shade of grey
When I want
You to be mine but not me to be yours
Is really fucked-up

Maybe I'm miserable
But so what
Doesn't anybody want that
The man comfortable at home
But not quite comfortable alone
Or not alone
Or ever really
No?

Fucking Charles Bukowski
That man saw it
That
Childlike despair
The stupid tantrums

And twisted logic
And base need to be
Desired

And mark my ego
Brand it hemophilia
Look at it gush maroon
On the beige
Look at it weep

Walk through the park
Of a life unlucky as me
And just see why the woe
From the twisted man hoe
Look upon dog corpses and criminal dads
The coinage corruption and gluttons greed
Fakers and faggots and it's all just me
The motherfucker
With baggage
Feeling endlessly
Belittled

Were it easier
If I'd just not
Survive
The clock's endless tick
Teases a final stop
Torment and tedium
The two life laws
That I've seen most prevalent
What if I said nay
Not today
Not tomorrow
Not ever

The final nail
To the casket of an
Over-talented underachiever
Nothing then

CLOGGED PIPES

I swear
To god
I'm far
From odd

It's just I got a bad case
Of clogged pipes

The shit don't flow
The stream is damned
The drain is blocked
The sponges crowd
The gates are closed
Tides are low
The hose is pinched
And ropes are knotted
The
God
Damn
Pipes are clogged

Just gotta plumb 'em
Myself
Unplug the plug
Unclog the honking cog
Fucking
Get it fixed you know?

The things in my head I mean
Those southern pipes run clean
I . . . assure you . . .
?

A Moth to a Flame

Tinder
Today's dating app
What a fucking dangerous place

Wired for dopamine
Making connections
Quicker and harder

I don't know what to do
When faced with multiple women
Who actually want to talk to me

Or at least have taken the time
To give me some attention
What do they get from me?

It makes me feel incompetent
Which doesn't help the impotence
And my short-fused irrationality

That feeling where you imagine
A life with another human
And what it could or might be like

It happens too much
Dozens of possibilities
And places to fuck up

Thinking and thinking and thinking some more
Like I'm some kind of man whore
Who could catch 'em all

It's dumb and I'm dumb
But like the moth I'm brought back to this
Fiery meeting place

Anything to forget the reality
That I just spend a dozen hours daily
Alone in front of a computer

I guess
But the worst part
Is that for the most part

The more you invest in it
The more it hurts when
The moth is consumed by the flame

Maybe that metaphor makes sense?

H

The rooms
And the walls
Don't mean anything really

The dirt
And the sky
May feel a little better but

The place I like to be is in arms
I think
Or I suppose

The cool that comes at a cost
Could everything get lost
Or just an afternoon

Cryptic right?
I know
It's just my ignorance I guess

But I'll speak to what I know
You've got me charmed
And I want to share a good day with you

I want to make you laugh
I want to engage your mind
I want that sweet chemical bliss

From two cozy cuddlers

A cool black-haired beauty
The human named H
Call me Cornell or Call Me A Dog

And I'll call you a Runaway
Cherry Bomb
Killer Queen

In Blue

Aa

Bonjour, Aa
It's not often that a
Guy like me gets the opportunity to
Write for someone as cool as you

So here's hoping I can find the right words

A woman in many ways immeasurable
She's more than a view that's pleasurable
She's a beautiful butterfly
With a story in her eye

You've thrown yourself to the wind
And so surprisingly it happened
That you've come across Kros
The boy who's always lost

I'd say my dream is to become a great man
But I don't exactly have a plan
So I'll say it now, for the next little while
My main goal in life is to make you smile

I'll write
I'll fight
I'll toil
And in the end I may foil
But I'm still going to try

To be a better guy
'Cause through the dating app fate
It's possible I've found someone great

If you like plants I'm sure you'll like me
I'm basically one-eighth of a tree

But like
No pressure
Who knows if we'd even enjoy each other's company
I guess for that we'll have to wait and see

And so until then
I'm in lesbian
With you
Aa

ADDICTIONS

Everyone's got their own
Some are healthy enough to be called habits
But the ones you don't want we all know as
Addictions

I got more than a few
On both sides of the line
And clustered in the middle
A mixed mix

The one I'm trying to put away
Is chocking my chicken
I can't be so
Sexually charged
I don't want to blow a fuse

The next I'm trying
Is these damn dating apps
It ain't right to scroll searching for
Fool's Aphrodite
And trying to find self-esteem

Lastly I really should cut back
On my green herb prayers
Unless I plan to use them
In a productive manner
That's how you make a habit

Anyways
twenty-two
I'd reckon somewhere in the top fifty
Of important years
I oughta do something with it

I oughta carve my own birthright
No longer a flaccid dynasty
This monument of a man
Will stand fully erect
Just gotta get better addictions

To the Girl Who Complimented My Face

Thanks!
It means a lot
And though we don't have much of a shot
I have to say you rock

Ca
The girl who's got guts
I could imagine her one punch
Could knock out a sucker's lunch

More than your average chick
She rockin' that Photoshop thick
And in a dress she's a wicked beauty
Were we not so far away if only

So *oui*
It's likely we
Will never meet
But I still think you're neat

Perhaps if the world is overrun by the undead
We can run away north far from dread
And find comfort from cuddles in bed
At least that's how I picture it in my head

Ca, we may never criss-Kros
Could even call it a kiss loss
But I'm smiling all the same
Because I appreciate your game

Thanks again for the compliment

22

Years on the earth
Still a dumb fuck
Who thinks swearing is cool
I'm chasing dopamine

My obsession
With women
Porn
And video games
Still shadow me

I've gotten better at
Being alive
For the most part
And I'm still learning
And I think I can exist in a world
That serves those
That know how to
Exploit

I'm still determined
To fix what those before me have broken
But the challenges grow

So here I am
Still taking it day by day
Here's hoping that the ideas in my mind

I can make real
And be worth a damn

And hey
Just maybe
I'll write something worth reading

MOST OF THE TIME

Most of the time it's just whatever
Just fucking whatever
You could write
You could play
You could beg
You could grovel
You could flirt
You could hang
You could be nice
You could do whatever

You do a lot of
Self-indulgent stuff
But you do, do
Good things for you

Doing whatever
Except what you can't
Like right now
You can't sleep
So you come back to this
Anti-vice device
Where you can play
And have something to say
And maybe people will pay
Someday

But most of the time I just do what I want
When I should definitely focus more on what's best

And I should absolutely go back to trying to get
Some
Rest
And enjoy sleepy time

NIGHTMARE

Candelabras in the halls
The widow in white
The ceiling is bleeding
And the ghosts ain't friendly

Lost
I don't have a clue
What I'm trying to do
Or what to say to you

But
If I were confined
To a world of nightmares
I'd hope you'd do the haunting

You seem hella cool
And I'm just a fool
From far away I shout
I like what you're about

So
Anyways
I hope well you fare
Girl of my nightmare

FOR THAT FAIRY

It's easy to get
Enthralled
In interesting people

We're all living our own lives
But these days
Fates collide
Dozen dames a day digitally

And so you see all sorts
And you meet all sorts
And it can get addicting

So I highly respect the woman
Who can shut shit down

Cla, I think you're cool
I mean
I've never met anyone before
Who's played the trumpet
On eight wheels
That's the kind of person
The world needs more of
At least
In my opinion

So I guess yeah
I hope we get along
'Cause if in your eyes I end up meh
I'm probably doing something wrong

FLIRTY POETRY?

I got to think of something funny
But all I can think of is Bunny
The embodiment of cool
Next to them I'd feel a fool

With hair in every colour
Dealing with every life bummer
If there's one thing I could tell her
I'd love to see her under pitter-patter
And kiss in the rain

But shit fuck and yuck
Who knows with my luck
Just thought I'd let you know
That I'm just a man hoe
Kinda lame and a little vain

But I think rats are awesome

STUFF AND THINGS

Doing stuff
Doing things
Trying those
Holding these
Getting with this
Or getting with that
Pinching it
Poking at
Rubbing what
And caressing such and rather
Just kinda
Doing stuff
And doing things

CHANGING RIGHT

The metaphor masters
And analogy artists
Have all said it before
About turning a page in life

Because it's really easy to think about life
Like you'd think of a book
What you've read, where you are, what you don't know
What you've done, what you're doing, what you don't know

Once the dreariness of the day to day
Starts to bottle up
The mechanisms of the mind
Pinch the page
And turn it over

Everyone's got a timer
For me it feels like every two months
Before the urges arise
I gotta shake it up
I gotta get in shape
I gotta find a new hobby
I should read more
I should write more
I should stop this and I should start that

It's a foolhardy endeavour
But one you gotta do
If you want to end up
Who you want to be in life
Or maybe it's just me

It feels like saying
Let's try and reinvent the train
After the tracks have been laid

But maybe I should stop with metaphorical ramblings
And think about what I want to see on this next page
'Cause if you're gonna make the effort
You should also put in the thought
To changing right

A Message for My Friend

I hope you're doing okay
I know you're not always
And you know I'm not always

I hope the slump is dumped
I hope one day we're living
Happy Interesting Lives

I hope we do cool shit with the time we get
And I hope downtime
Isn't damning time

I hope you're doing okay
B
I trust time to bring a better day

IT'S BEAUTIFUL

In my head
In the imaginary park
Next to the imaginary path
On the imaginary bench
Sits the imaginary me
Using imaginary smooth moves
On an imaginary girl
She's everything that makes dopamine
And her earrings are extravagant

Then there's the real me
High above the imaginary clouds
Crying like a castrated god
For he knows his reality's been consumed by advertising

I must grow
I can't let sacrificed limbs lie in vain

Not Here

No that's not my bed it's just where I sleep
No that's not my food it's just what I eat
No that's not my girl it's just who I fuck
No that's not my head it's just where I think

An empty skull filled with lead
Scars and wounds that all warn dread
Flowers on a frilly dress
Covered in coats of a noir paint

Sinking birds and lions without pride
Just some boring American tour guide
I have but one thing to you confide
This isn't the first time that I've tried

To fit a square peg in a circular hole

NOT DOING TOO GOOD

You know
It's really hard for me
Not to see the same faulty
Manners
That I share with my folks
The anger
The narcissism
The blissful ignorance
And the crushing self-doubt
I'm sometimes astounded by their
Fortune from misfortunes
Maybe this mistake's got what it takes
To overcome the high bar
And flop into a placing finish
At the top
With all the other broken stair climbers
Looking for a slice of heaven
That doesn't exist on this earth

BROTHERS

Let me tell you something about my brother
I don't talk about him a lot, but I think a lot about him

He's a good kid
Looking for happiness
He's a hard worker
Takes care of his kids

He does dumb shit sometimes
If I could borrow a phrase
He's good a curious thinker
Especially when it comes to combustion

I think in a way we're both nomads
Broken kids from broken homes
Always moving and trying to hold down on the past
The thing that often stops us
And puts us in our place
Is the women
We find company
I guess if I was a dog
I'd say he's a wolf
But really I just imagine
A mean coyote

Nonsense

Whoever said honesty is the best policy
Probably doesn't think very much
I can think of a million truths a second
That shouldn't be shared
Honesty is a fine policy
But it won't get you very far
A better policy would be
Speak truthfully when justice calls
And speak what should be said,
What they want to hear
The rest of the time

Just let the river flow
No use digging sticks into rocks

LIKE A

Like this
Like that
Everything's gotta be like something else
You know what today was like
Crap
You know what life is like
Shit
From the earth
And straight back to it

A Poem in a Park

White widow
The melted snow
Covers the ground around me
How could this be
'Tis a season's end prematurely
It's not a good sign

Such a busy park
A man with high risk just walked by

"And that's why I told them to get out,
'Cause I got that letter from my doctor
And they put me on the high risk
You know I had to tell the GM"

He's got a good four-legged companion
And a friend by his side

A man more than past the halfway bend
Looks at the public gym
Maybe on a whim
Or maybe the start of a comedy or tragedy

Four-man disk golfers
And knee-high scooter walkers
And me
A confused guy

Off to the side
I wonder if it's Frisbee Friday

Anyways
I've not much yet to say
Last I'll say be thy
The coming days' prophesies
That the end of my free time is nigh
So let me say one last midseason's goodbye
To this park
And my broke-bitch blues

CLOSE WALLS

Through my portcullis
I see a shallow sea
And a net
Hewn brown

My other crewmates
Are all ghosts
With a taste
For the finer things

I can feel the draft
The floorboards are creaking
It won't be long
Before the great sinking

We've dug up the sea
For all its treasure and pearls
And now we must succumb to
Our barren new world

In my small box
I dream of a vast space
But my air is running thin
I hope I can rise from below

Direct the wayward spinning wheel
Onto a course of consideration

As to what
Needs
To be done

We're running out of miracles

BATTLEFIELD

The Blackfoot
V
Cree
Battle

A final test of might
Between two peoples
While being decimated continuously
By the white man

The Blackfoot rained rifle fire from above
A tactical outwitting
The Cree ran to the river
And then there was nowhere to flee

If only history favoured
The other side
Perhaps there'd be more tales
Of battles between great tribes
Rise and falls of mighty peoples
The great stories of Big Bear
But no
Instead we get a long list
Of exploiters and profiteers
With names like John

What's so great
About our bridges and balconies
If all they bring
Is death

Just a bunch of ants trying to look big

THINKERS

Anyone want to take care of this?
The puddle's starting to reach the carpet
Any moment now
Things will abruptly change
The profound nature of society
Is long overdue for a great shift
A shattering

The borders
Of great empires
On maps
Used to be a good way of telling
What the world crisis was
But the maps are useless now

The burning forests tell more
Than the paper they die for
Than the people in the homes made of their flesh

Next time why don't you stand over your dumpster fire and
inhale all the fumes
Instead of forcing that reality on the defenceless

Production has never been higher!
Is that as far as our capacity for thinking goes?

We've grabbed the anchor
And can't let go
An addiction
To a false form of life

We are a disease
I don't see the difference
Between a fever killing the flu
And the climate controlling
Resource viruses

Those damned and dirty fucks that take everything and give
nothing back. The cowards in mansions paying wages to an
army of suckers.

Just let it end
We don't deserve this land

The great climate culling is coming
And the thinkers have been defeated by the dense

STARS

Make a wish
See them twinkle
Those beautiful
Exploding
Flashes

Oh how the stars inspire dreams
Far-flung acts of fiery defiance
In a cold dark universe
A light so bright guides the way

The stars see me pass the eve
They shine softly into my gentle goodnight
If there's one place I'd want to have my
Last breath
It'd be among the unfathomable
Celestial flares of death

SAVAGES

On a warm autumn day
The children are out to play

Running along the fallen leaves
Are scores of tiny savages

Screams
And shouts
Endless explosions of emotions

The base
And raw
Core
Of humans
Exemplified

And even now
They're learning
The meaning
Of wanting

They want to play
They want to have fun
They want to win
They want to want

And they'll always be wanting more

Truly it is a miracle
That we haven't devoured this planet yet
And been spit out
By our gross incompetence

We'll always be tiny savages in over our head

I should get a dog

KIDS WITH PHONES

I see these kids
With old iPhones
In thick cases
That bike around
This side of town

It sorta reminds me
Of a chimpanzee

They flick it on
Answer the phone
And always asks
Who is this

They don't have a care
About the other side

The box it rings
Answer it I must
It probably signals
A sign of trust

It's weird to say
But how small their minds

I once remember
A time like that

But
Not a lot

A few memories
Dot the place
I was always anxious
About my face

SOMETHING

Anything
A drunken scrawl
A rat with ink on his tail
A particularly poignant elephant

Just get it down
The gorilla on his birthday
The boy with the balloon in the McDonald's
The pizza girl who can't make it to the door

As long as
You fall in love
You get too high
You cry in the bathroom

It means something
When you can't get out of bed in the morning
When you can't make a smile
When your arm falls asleep

They'll have it
For the radical movements
For the new generation
For the thirsty toads

After you die
Say goodbye

Say happy birthday
Say it

So many words
So many meanings
So many wasted lines
So many quiet spaces being filled with noise

In the age of advertise me
Nobody's free
We've traded silence for shouts
And reasoning for Ignorance

I have my doubts
In fact I don't think we have long
Let the ghosts of men with vision
Press that big red button

Or let us raise hell on earth
And get mouth burn from Satan's cum
Let's make a world
Where death truly means mercy

Maybe someday
I'll say something
That'll put me
In a position to do something

But people only want to give the crown
To those who lie
And say they don't want it
I'm not that kind of liar

I believe in my greed
My envy of a good deed

Let me change our earth's ways
Let me be the symbol for better days

. . .

Or go to hell
Or
Something

Tomorrow Yesterday
or in Between

What's the point of making sense of things

Men play bagpipes in filled parks
A goblin buys a pizza and breaks hearts
A tower of gold
Argues a tower of silver

Wisdom is destroyed
And patience forgotten
Gratification becomes addicting
And sadness is sold to the broke

The world is a big cookie
And it's going to crumble
Even the gluttonous will starve then
But they'll last longer than most

The elves will run to the trees
Whores and nuns on their knees
And the pope
Will pray to man

It sure beats not being able to bank on Sundays
It sure beats waiting for the horse rider

It sure beats having to plow the fields
It sure beats having to hunt or be hunted

But who knows if it does
Guess I should do my homework

A Shadow

Or should I say
My shadow
My
Oldest friend

For as long as I can remember
I always thought
That the only thing I'd keep
Throughout my life
Is my shadow

I've tried to make that not so
I've held on to
Things
Friends and family
Lovers
But I lose them all in the end
But not my shadow

He's all too loyal of a companion
A commitment to
Dark feelings
And dark thoughts

He's a good friend
He wants nothing other than
To stick to me

And I like that about it
I don't have to worry
I don't have to seek him out
He's just there

Me my shadow and I
We'll go everywhere I'm sure
I just can only hope
It's not just the lonely two of us
Because I can't share with him
My
Excitement and joy
My sorrow and tears
He can't hold me
And tell me things will be fine

And there's nothing I can do for him
And there's so much I want to do
With someone
Who could replace my shadow

GREEN-HAIRED GIRL

What are the odds

I've met a girl
Who shares the name of an ex
Who shares the hometown of an ex
Who shares the marijuana fascination of an ex
Who shares the dream job of an ex

Who has a kid
Just like my ex

But you're not my ex
You've got green hair
And it's not fair
For me to compare

The moment
Things went wrong
Was when I fell for her
When I wanted something real

So I ask you
M
Can this all be fake
Can we live in a dream world
Where cuddles and good company
Can exist

A mere time
Where
We just
Chill and have fun
And resolve to the idea
That a time will come
Where we may never see each other again
Is that alright with you?

If not
Don't let me waste your time
You've got a family on the line
Legs that blow my mind
A true kind of beauty, divine
In every kind of way, so fine
And I'm just after what is mine
That I don't yet have

WHOOP-UP DRIVE

It's rush hour
Humpday
I'm on a
Dry
Grassy
Knoll
To my right
In the distance
I can see downtown
Covered in smoke
Across the street
That's filled with traffic
There's a church
A building with no business
To my left the road stretches on
To places parks and plazas
I can't see

Hundreds of people
Pass me by
They can all see me
Quite clearly I feel
But I can hardly see
A handful
They each have their own box
On wheels
A floating sanctuary

That brings them all
Freedom
And privacy

Some are old
Some are new
Some are well washed
And some are well used
I think that one was European
I saw one earlier that was yellow
And in it a girl who looked like
A wasp

There's a Jeep
My mom used to drive one of those
There's a van
Caked in dirt

There's something about traffic
That doesn't sit right with me
So much energy
Being used
So so so many people
Alone surrounded by three seats
And just
So many people
So far apart

I hope I learn something
From my time sitting on
The end of Whoop-up Drive

The Old-School Fool

Look at that old-school fool go
The guy who gets nostalgic
For things that haven't reached the end yet

What a sad son of a bitch
Who spits on the bugs
That crawl between his toes

What a mad motherfucker
Who'll never understand
Because there's someone on the other side of the glass

Look at the loner
The one that spends all his time
Thinking about the people he doesn't spend time with

What a wasted space
It's no wonder everyone that comes near this place
Walk out in brisk pace

What a loss of words
Written digitally and will be lost
This is a failed post-mortem medium

Look at this guy
Look into my brown eyes
And tell me I'm worth love

Even though this heart won't beat
Even though all I feel is greed
Even though all I want is devotion

Even though all I can do
Is try
And
Fail

SULTRY

She's got the devil in her eyes
And good lord some beautiful thighs
Wearing sexy black panties
Like some kind of fantasies

Fair
With red hair
I seem to be sucked in
By the sultry K

I don't think my words do justice
For what would happen if it were just us
Not to be too forward or callous
But I want to make the rabbit jealous

I admire the fauna
Tattooed on ya
There's an ocean I want to drown in
I want to feel the hold of the Kraken

Those are my thoughts for the girl
Who got my message of me about to unfurl
So if in the streets or the sheets you want to twirl
I bet you'd rock my world

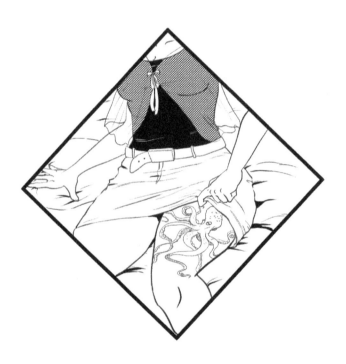

What a Night

One night
Stand

What's with life anyways
What does it want from us
Does it just want us
To find a spot
To just be dumb
And have fun

The bed was a-bouncing
And the night was arousing
But from where did this night come from
Was it the brownies, was it just dumb
Luck

From two souls looking to
Fuck

I'm going to remember this
For a long time
I feel
I felt
Alive

THE PIGEON AND THE DUCK

Quack
Quack quack
Quack quack quack quack quack quack quack quack quack
quack quack quack quack quack quack

Coo
Coo coo

Quack quack?
Coo coo

Coo coo coo coo coo coo coo coo coo coo!
Quack quack quack quack quack quack quack!
Coo coo coo coo coo coo coo coo coo coo!
Quack quack quack quack quack quack quack!

Quack
Coo

DON'T JUDGE

Today
I told a money
Hungry hoe
That I was going to cut my dick off
She just wanted to make sure
I logged on correctly

MAN OF THOUGHT

Put that in my epitaph
I may not be aware of
The happenings of another's mind
Bet let it be known thusly
That I
Am a man of thought

Sometimes I think about boobs
And sometimes I think about theory
But thinking I am
And doing
I'm often not

My thoughts can be crippling
My thoughts can be revealing
I think my thoughts control me
More than is healthy

I'm thinking right now
Of a man
Doing his studies
Writing the words
Written in front of him
Absorbing
Information

I'm thinking of a man
In conversation
He thinks about
The last conversation
And there's a reference
In this conversation
That he can make about
The last conversation

I imagine a man
With boundless
Confidence and discipline
Ruling his world
A man of action
Suave and charismatic
And he does what he can
To help who he knows

I think I'm a man
Of many different hats
But when it comes down to it
I can be a miserable sod
Sometimes I just need to feel
A little
Je ne sais quoi
Do I dare say love
When I'm not quite sure what it means
Perhaps
Maybe I just feel
That I need someone to make me better
Because I can only go so far alone

Want me?

What
You want me?
The lazy bum who sleeps in till three
The fuck who isn't worth a damn
The needy asshole who wants all your time
The dumbass who just gets sad and can't do anything about it
Nobody wants me
And neither do you
So why would you get my hopes up

Weathering Blue

Sugary foods
And solitude
Bad dates
And missed connections

Distant family
Lost opportunity
Enfeebled
Body and mind

Misplaced memories
Lost lust
Righteous wrongdoings
And an expanded capacity
For fucking up

Fading dreams
Draining wallets
Crying children
Lying on stiff cushions

Sad rhymes
Boring times
Angry Men
In empty den

Just another day
Weathering Blue
Just my kinda way
Of wasting every nice day

It'd make me really glad
To find everyone secretly sad
Does that make me bad
Maybe just a tad

But fuck it
Just like all my other wasted words
I can't manifest into being
Something great
With just writing something clever
Rejuvenate
I hope you have a relaxing day
I hope your worries wash away

If you need anything from me
Don't hesitate to ask Ke
For drugs
For treats
For hugs
For meats
For today it is my desire
That you face no ire

I'm only one message away
I hope you have a relaxing day

HEADLIGHTS

It must be scary for a deer
To see heaven
And be blinded by it
To have it consume your world

Of course
The headlights
Or heaven
That I get lost in
Aren't so blinding
Thank god

And the headlights I get lost in
Aren't weightless
They aren't ethereal
They're
A part of a whole
A whole I know nothing about
And so I write
For the headlights

And by God
Are they glorious

WALKING IN OLD SHOES

A 10:00 a.m. purple sunrise
Dawn's over the path
That a short-sighted greedy man
Walks alone

He thinks he's not alone
He sees someone else with his soul
But he's just walking in worn-down footpaths
Wearing old shoes

The air is chilled
But his heart beats warm
His hands are deep in his jacket
Otherwise they'd fall off

Innocence Ignorance and bliss
Hand in hand in hand
But they're bound to trip
Walking in old shoes

Nothing will make you grow older
Quicker
Than just one take
At heartbreak

REMOVING NEGATIVITY

There's a belief
A way of life
That if you cut out
The bad things in life
You'll live better

Cut out the bad people
De
Toxify
Eat less junk
Consume less drugs
Live naturally
Or whatever

I think the line
That's hardest to cross
Is cutting out
Your old self
I mean that's the goal right?
To be someone new
You can't be who you used to be

In the end I feel
Most of my life
Has just been a series
Of becoming someone else
Never

Satisfied
Always
Removing
And replacing

SUPPOSEDLY

This girl Rory
Has been brought into
My field of view

And supposedly
This girl Rory
Has a pen and mind
That can sass my grind

And supposedly
This girl Rory
With a knack for rhyme
Thinks I look fine

And supposedly
This girl Rory
Might really show me
What it means to be lucky

And supposedly
This girl
Rory

Might have just made this young thing
Swoon

Bonjour, mademoiselle

It's very nice to meet you
I hope you feel it too
And maybe stay a spell

Supposedly
This girl Rory
Might just be
Too good for me

WICKED SMILE

I think I've just seen
The greatest smile
I've ever seen
I must be some kind of lucky

My worried esteem
Always has me questioning
But I'd do anything
Just to see her beam

A blue-haired beauty
Who thinks I'm cool
She'll learn I'm a fool
I'm glad we shared tea

Let's live
Let's die
Let's love
and let's cry

You and me
That's art I see
Let's turn this world into a canvas
And let our memories paint the pages

And don't worry
My words aren't meant to hurry
But I just want to say this
I want to see you more, miss

HOLD THE POSE

That's it
Just right there
For a moment
I thought I looked cool
Then I twitched
And lost my nerve
What a stupid
Way to go

Just don't fucking worry about it
Even the best can lose composure
Just breathe.
Appreciate
The
Moment.

At Every Turn

Failure
Failure here
And failure there
I've even failed with my hands before
You just got to give up
And try again
And when you're done doing that
. . .
My ass is sore on the concrete
And my frown doesn't wanna go away
But I'm still here
Just another day

FALLING LOOKS GRACEFUL

Falling
From the sky
Your whole world shattering
You
In a delusional panic
Scared of the ground
But only you can see the impending doom
To the onlookers
There is only grace
Even a limp corpse can flap in the wind
Until you hit the ground
To them
You're flying
So don't you worry too much about your fall

NUMBNESSNESS

Passing time
Smoking dope
Chasing girls
Looking for work
Watching sports
Watching TV
Thinking about money
Baking sweets
Eating
Melting in the sun
Walking parks
Skating sidewalks
Driving nowhere
And listening to the radio
Not a bad way to go
Writing thoughts
Playing songs
Dreaming of
Making
A
Dif-fer-ence
And now I think I'm
Singing the blues
Just a guy
Underground
Wearing the shoes
Of 1972

Still just trying
To make some kinda
Difference
Looking to the year
Of 2022

The Other Side of 4:00 AM

Stupid ass
Infatuations
Lame fucking
Let downs

A vacuum
Bigger than the void
And responses
Not given

Thoughtfulness
Nonexistent
Cry baby
Chirp to the deaf

Alone
And ignored
And wishing
For genuine affection

Smite and perish
Damn and condemn
Wicked
Loveless liars

And show me something real
Or show me

Anything
At all

Three acute angles
Surround the hollow thorn in my side
I feel sick
It's all the sugar

So here's to swallowing the nail
And seeing what the iron does
They say
You got to strike when hot

Maybe it's the clock
But right now I feel like
My only option is to suffer
I don't know how to make things better

I don't know what I can ask of you

This lame brain's always been better
At creating fiction than seeing fact

So you like me now
What if I crack
And say something mean
Will you come back

If I take the tape off my mouth
And call shit manure
Do I lose my mystique
My boring boy demure

At some point you'd have to see
Me on the other side of 4:00 a.m.

So
I hope you'll still go out with me

Kindest regards,
Kros Dyck

GROWING YOUNGER

When I was twenty-one
I ate a bug
To impress a girl

When I was eight
I did math
To impress a girl

This merry-go-round is making me dizzy

Trade's Girl

Trade's girl tales
Signal males
An unserious forte
Matched me today

Wicked breadwinner
Looking for a sinner
To show practice in
More than just hammerin'

I'd know what to say
If this was all just play

But frowns lie on two crowns

What Are you Looking For?

Well I guess in life the only thing I'm really looking for is
To make the best of what I got

But that's not what you're asking isn't it

Well if I asked an asshole he might say
What the fuck kinda question is that
Who fucking knows
I'm trying to make the most of my days
I want to take chances
I want some new shit

An anxious person might say
That's exactly not what I'm looking for
I want someone to feel safe with

The optimist would certainly say
I'm looking for love
Shoot for the moon
Fall in the stars

And the sad boy would say
I'm just looking to feel
Something

Hell if I were to ask an existentialist
He'd tell me

He's just looking
For is irrelevant

So
What
Am
I
looking for

Something
With someone
That's mutually beneficial
In a special
Kind of
Way

So love
I guess

Oh
And some
Fun
Raunchy
Sex please too
Thanks
I'm a pretty horny motherfucker

Self-portrait in the style of Bukowski

A womanizer
And a stoner
Who can't get a boner
Lost in the fridges
And between fence posts
Looking for the ladder
That doesn't exist
I cast ghastly gaze
To haze and warn
Beware the bastard born
And leave the lonely kid
Alone
To fester and grow
Terrible thoughts
Of living dreams
That aren't his
Endlessly sharpening
Useless tools

THE BOY WITH THE BLACK BALLOON

She actually gave me the idea for this
So let's hope it doesn't disappoint

Real talk
Cheap food
An impromptu connection
Leading to a ten-hour
Serotonin erection

Pictures don't do justice
The girl who's had time in the rains
Who comes from
A belief above

Flying the friendly skies

I love
How we got to sit and read
Poetry

'Cause commonality can
Do double double Diddley
And it's nice
Not being alone

Ki
I'm sorry the dove love died

And I promise my best
To try not to hurt you

See the sea seed is sown
And fates flung it far from home

And I'm looking forward to watching it grow

I hope you can stomach
My
Boringnessnesses

Yakety-yak
And a boy with a black balloon

My Morbid Curiosity

Death's weird
In the same way
Life's weird

We live
And
We die

You're not really
Dead before
You're alive

But you sure are
After
You're alive

I've seen death
I've seen dead
Bugs
Mice
Frogs
Birds
A lot of birds
Fish
Rabbits
Cats
Goats

Dogs
People
Deer
Cows
Bears Prairie dogs
And
Di
No
Saurs

The most recognizable
Things about death
Are
The sights
And sounds

You'll absolutely
Hear death
More often than witness it

The sounds of a scuffle
A growl
A yelp
A woosh
A slam

THE WILD CAT IN A BOX

Don't scratch my balls
Don't scratch my balls
Please for the love of God
Don't scratch my balls

Feral
And wild
Is the cursed cat
That I must bring to a witch doctor

The curse
Is a shot-gunning
Of too many
Offspring
The amount of which
Is a function
Of an exponential growth
Of a factor of at least three
Or maybe four

But the curse also
Lies in the beastly males
That come out
To chase the heat

But there's not a lot we can do about them
And thus

The cat
In the box

The cat timidly steps through the threshold
And a subtle
Rattle
Scares him into the trap
With a thud
The plan succeeds
And a life
Short-lived so far
Flashes into this creature's eyes

And panic ensues

Jump!
And immediately
Smack!
She crashes into the cage
Dazing
And
Stopping

And after the immediate
Flight response
Comes the cold
Fearless feral
Cat

Scratching
And digging
And jumping again
Anything to get out

And all I can do is coo
And offer my calmest
Reassurance
I know this must be scary

She's calm now
I hope
In a cage
In a room
With some food
And a place to poo

Sleep tight
Tomorrow
Will be scary
And beyond your realm
Of understanding

CLOSING THE WELL

There comes a time
When the toxins grow
And the nourishing water
Becomes tainted
And you have to close the well

Even if rainfall brings cleaner waters
Or you tasted it last week
And it was just fine
Don't be weak
Close the well

You've spent too much time
Drawing life from one hole
At some point
You have to let the well
Fall behind
As you March ahead

You've tried your water treatments
And know they don't work
You aren't the scientist
That you think you are
Close that well
and find your something
Somewhere new

THE SMALL-TOWN REGISTRY OFFICE

Every
Driver's test
Licence renewal
Vehicle registration
I've ever done
Has been in my
Small-town
Registry office

The nice ladies
Running the double front desk
Have probably worked here
As long
As I
Have been alive

They'll probably still be here
After I'm gone too

And of course my mother
Went and got pissed of
By the simple power

Of the government worker
Saying
No

I think it's a neat office

Don't Feel Like Satan

Why does it feel awful
To do the right thing
To hurt someone
And lose
For the betterment of both

Why is it so easy
To pretend everything is okay

I know it's no use
To replay the past
It just sucks
Because
I still don't know
What went right
And
What went wrong

A slew of stupid mistakes
With
Fun
Dripped in

To much honesty
And not enough
Company
Wrong place wrong time

It's a fool's errand
To try to make a pretty woman smile
When you're not
What she's
Looking
For

And what's the point
If she couldn't get the reference
I don't feel like Satan
But I am to her

Hopeless
Romantic
Tragic
Selfishness
Wrapped up
In a
Long-haired hippy
Antagonistic asshole
Lost looking longingly
For love

With low self-esteem
At least she might get that one

THE MCDONALD'S PLAYPEN

I find it very
Very strange
That one memory that I remember bliss from
Was in a pen filled with
Screams
And messy
Sticky surfaces

In the McDonald's Playpen
With a girl I really liked
Her daughter
And an absolutely chaotic
Random
Mix of middle
To lower
Income families

I felt no competition
The energy
That fuels
My need to be better
Was gone
I was among
The weak and weary
I only felt
Solidarity
With my fellow man

Surrounded by
The young
The innocent
The loud
And mean
They just don't know any better

And so I sit alone
In my usual introverted self
Gently perceiving my surroundings

And I'm happy

One day
I'll gladly start a family
But for now I thank
Everyone who's let me
Join theirs

It was
Loud and annoying
And I think at the time
That's the message that made it
To my mouth
I wish the cold outside
Was a good excuse
For my cold inside

But that would mean I can't make it better
And I know I can

You would never believe me
If I told you I really enjoyed that day

And I think that was a big reason I don't think we'd ever
Work
But I believe in the power of
Time
If it's meant to be it'll be
And if it's not
Well that's the reality I write from now

After we left
In the cold wind
And the quiet
Noisy
Bus ride
My memory is hazy
But I think
I didn't meet
Some invisible standards
From the
Unaware judge
That hides in your skull

I wonder if I'm so mean to you
Because I
Want
So bad
To be better

Because the care I was given
Was harsh
But I learned from it

But I'm just justifying the words of an asshole
The same words were said to me

I don't know what's right or wrong
But I didn't think about any of that
In the McDonald's Playpen

In that
Room of rampant rowdy reckless
Silly shouting sad mad
Carefree kids
I felt alive
And in the moment

And I believed I could be a good dad
At least
Better than the ones before me

I hope you and your
Flower
blossom

And in case I haven't said enough
Thanks for letting me into your garden
And sorry
For spitting on the daisies

COLD HANDS WARM
HEART AND THE CLOCK

She came at the best time
When my perspective was so small
And the world I lived in
Was so
Small

In a time
When I was scurrying with a mouse
I had a chance meeting
With a dancer

I'm glad
That as far as I know
My honesty
Didn't hurt you
Because
I know
It's hurt others

How do people make other people better
I suppose is my question for it all

I remember under the stars
I felt nervous
But like a prince all the same

And
She liked how I danced
And
She liked my heart
And
I liked her art
And
I liked how
She seemed so put together
While I was falling apart

But I already know my perspective is small

Oh to dance in the halls once more
Oh to rock the bed
I think your patience is something I never deserved
But I appreciate it all the same

A sun to shine in a harsh winter

A friend that finds itself manifested in time
I know you had a proverb for that
Wise and worldly
The girl that drives for miles and miles

But I've spilled enough words on the page
I hope we see each other again
Soon
In a new age

COLD HANDS WARM HEART

She came at the best time
When my perspective was so small
And the world I lived in
Was so
Small

In a time
When I was scurrying with a mouse
I had a chance meeting
With a dancer
At the time it felt like
I was mirroring the mouse
The mouse want not
For monogamy
So

An actor and an actress meet
Through a mutual friend
For a school project
And chemistry was created

Everything was honest
At least I never kept secrets
Although I do believe
All
Would
Be

Better
If I lied

Oh well

How do people make other people better
I suppose is my question for it all

I remember under the stars
I felt nervous
But like a prince all the same
And
She liked how I danced
And
She liked my heart
And
I liked her art

But the chemistry
I think
Wasn't fully there
I think
I was too busy falling for someone else

Someone else's
Laugh
Smile
Eyes and brows
Hair
Bum
Tongue

I think it's funny-sad
How once you asked
What my type was
And if you asked today
I'd say you

Oh well

I just hope we're all better
Than we were before

Now I must attend to the
Dog with the mud on my bed

EMBERS

The tired
Last lights
Of the flames
Burn out
As your eyes close

The memory of a night
Shared in memory of
A collective
Future
Story

What does the end feel like?
Sad.

The acceptance of what
Did
And did not
Unfold

But the time spent
Living
Is always
Worth being there for

Just looking for
The right vibes

The music's wrong
The conversation's off
Where's the dreams
Of what could be

The end of a fun night

SEPTUM

Across the entire piercing spectrum
I think the one I like most is the septum

A curious bridging of holes

A symbol
Directly
In
Front

A sign of strength
A fearless fact
A hella hot
Adornment

The balance between beauty and beast
Made to be worn
By the kind
That sees

Both sides of the coin

But I just think it's neat

SHADOW BOXED

Fists
Fly
To the rhythm
And beat
Angst triumphed
By passion
Far goes the man
With the drum and plan
Thump thump
If you want to go fast go alone
If you want to break the glass
You'll be hard pressed to find company
If you want someone special
Let luck lash you repeatedly
And see if you can win the wheel
Feeling fire
Futile
When surrounded by trees
And there's nowhere to run
Ninety days spent
Suffering in bliss
Thirty days left
A countdown to create a new man
But now
I'm boxed in
And fists fly at shadows
And weeds would mock

And grow along the burning lead
Dormant disaster does threaten
Thresholds
A fool who thinks words are cool
Surrounded by
Unbeknownst critics
Why does it have to be funny
Why does funny have to be
The be all end all
Why make you laugh
When you can cry catharsis
What's so interesting about the madman
What's so interesting about it all
Can't we just shut up and look at each other
Why's that so hard

I hate Tinder because it's a game of missed connections
Fuck you tell me I'm pretty
Rip out my hair and read me one of my poems
Let me lick your face
Sit silently and enjoy the scenery
I'll compete for anything and everything
So call me a winner
And see the empty place
Behind my face
Watch it flood and drain
My information brain
Angry sad apathy
All wrapped up
In the boring me
A mess I confess
Shooting for the top
So tag along move on or revolve
Sorry
I'm just tired

Just a medium that serves as a shovel
Trying to dig the hole
That leads to the cave
That leads to the tunnel
That leads to the seed
That meaning is made of

Ask me for a poem
Ask for something specific or don't
Help me feel like I'm not a sack of shit
Thanks
Love,
Kros

THE BROKEN SHUTTERED WINDOW

For the past few months
I've ridden past
On a bike
A broken shuttered window

I see a light
That blinks every few days
When I ride past
That broken shuttered window

I can't see well
The other side obscured
But I see that light
And I know someone must be in there

I call out
To that blinking light
I ask simply
Do you spend a lot of time with that light?

I get a brief reply
No
What about you
And your bike

I do spend a lot of time on this bike
Probably more than I should
I think to myself
I guess it feels nice trying to get somewhere
When you're not going anywhere

Unsatisfied with that brief conversation
I call out to the light again
Light on the other side of the window
Do you enjoy your life?

It's an honest question
I can't see what it's like
On the other side of that
Broken shuddered window

I wait
And wait
And wait a little longer
And then I leave

I ride past that
Broken shuttered window
And I see it blink
It's little light

And the days
Weeks
And months
Roll by

I stop by the window again
There's a smoke
With a familiar smell
And so I ask

It was a big question
I understand
Let me now ask
Your favourite kind of grass

And the window is silent
It's light still blinks
My bike I still ride
And the days go by

Filling a Day

I spend every moment
Trying to figure out
What to do next
What a dumb way
To fill the day

Why can't I
Just
See
What
The
Day
Will
Bring

There's a beaver in that pond over there
A brown spot
In a grey pond
Amongst a see of green
I bet if I get closer he'll slap his tail at me

Stepping on ants
Like some twisted god
But they don't die
And that just makes me feel sad
And angry
What could have been merciful

Has turned wicked
There is no grey
Just a flailing ant
On a black sheet
I stepped on him again
And he disappeared
His sole reaped
His graceless goodbye
Stepped on by
Some twisted god

I don't like to think about what God is
I try to focus on what's in front of me
It's important
To see the small
And smile

MY FIRST

It was my first relationship
You understand
I had to make sure
That I made
Every
Stupid
Mistake
In the book

Not on purpose mind you

I don't use my words
With war on the mind
But I should really
Watch how I speak
My mouth moves
And then
My brain
But that's not all bad
It's part of who I am

It something real I think

Anyways that's a long-winded way
To say
I said some mean shit

But I felt safe doing that
'Cause it was never real
I don't think I could ever
Live in your den of shadows

THE MYSTIC MOUSE

We were a branch cut short for the safety of the sidewalk
A tagged fish that could track a school
An old building seen on the horizon
And you couldn't tell if it stood tall

It was the mystic and a kid with a K
Living the only immoral way
Sin and sadness lie in the wake
Of the mouse with a spoiled birthday cake

Hoard your people, be they big or small
I only met you this fall
You chewed me up, spit me out
But there was glue on the top of your mouth

There's a sword in my hand and noose on the floor
I'll be gone before you know it, I don't mean to bore
There's a whole world you're missing from your
underground den
Try making a friend with just that glowing pen

The dirt beneath you would look right on top
This ain't about the things you bought
I got words I ain't going to say to your face
But could you please vacate my mental space

I got the nerve and the time to rhyme
About when you threw me away for a lime
I see the shit stain on your wall of memory
There's a grin hanging there that's what I see

Maybe next time you'll learn the fact
Was that turning the knife was all you lacked
but I know you ain't one for learning
So watch as your world keeps turning

Life is what you make it
And by God I swear I'm gonna make it

She said she had a third eye that could help her see
But I know you can't see outside the light
You bumped into me in the dark and said it was on purpose
But I know you don't know where you're going

RUNNING IN THE HALLWAY

In a four-walled world filled with rules
I always wanted to break some with you
A simple dash down the lane
What I'd give to run down that hall again

Nervous and anxious and boisterous and fun
I shoulda taken your hand for that run
A memory tainted by regret and pain
What I'd give to run down that hall again

Life's a risk, leave everything to chance
I promise next time I won't be scared to dance
I won't hold back, I'll look up in the rain
I'll make sure I run down that hall again

Another Asshole's Apology

I spent the first eighteen years of my life
Believing I was on the brink of bankruptcy
So sorry if I'm a little money conscientious

I spent the first twenty years of my life
Having never touched a woman
And then I discover that my dick can't get hard
When I want it to
So sorry if I focused on sex too much

I grew up in an angry household
With an overworked mother
And a dad with daddy issues that'll never resolve because
his dad's dead
So sorry if I called you a slut

I've never felt safe in any of my relationships
I've lost a lot of friends
And family
And missed a lot of chances for happiness out of fear
So sorry if I'm a bit needy

I come from a big family of teenage parents
And I've seen ambition and drive

Burn to dust in people's souls
And I feel like my birth
Was just another couple's roadblock
So sorry your child scares me

And I've never
Ever
Looked into someone's eyes
And saw eternity
So sorry for falling in love

And I'm sorry
That I thought
We could grow together
And overcome our personal problems
As a unit
What a fucking stupid idea

You want to know why I think you're a slut
I broke up with you knowing that I couldn't be
What you wanted me to be
My ambition won't allow it
And like the fucking selfish asshole that we both
know
You
Are
You seduced me
Waiting for me by the bus
Adding fuel to a stupid fantasy
That one day I'd come to a place
That I could safely call home
And you'd be waiting for me

So I'm sorry
For being a selfish angry asshole
I tried to warn you

I think if I knew then what I know now
The outcome would still be the same

I Was Just A Crumb

I am a crumb
A part of a whole
A left-behind remnant
Of some food that was probably delicious

The crumb lives a solitary life
I exist in my habitat
I live within my habits
But I yearn for everything and all

And one day a mouse
With hunger in her eyes
And greed in her stomach
Spotted this curious crumb

And she came to the crumb's home

It would take a thousand years
To write all that happened
In the next four months
That's a lot in crumb time

But the mouse grew bored
And the hunger was still there
So it ate the crumb whole
And washed me down with slime

I suppose I saw this coming
Thought I the foolish crumb
I guess this is it then
I'm resigned to this den

The digestion process was messy
As the crumb lost his form
And he could no longer see
The mouse that ate he

Then the natural cycle occurred
I saw a light at the end of the tunnel
I was pushed toward it
And in the sunlight I discovered

Well you get the metaphor

The lowest of the low
Not chewed up and spit out
But to be swallowed and shat
Does it get worse than that

Now that I'm somewhere new
Does that mean I can be someone new
It occurred to me then
That I was on dirt-covered ground

It's time to grow
It's time to change
It is of this earth
I'll be reborn again

A process that takes time
But it's one that's worth

All the sorrow seen
I shall become the earth

Though it's silly to say
I am no longer poo
It's the natural way
To become something new

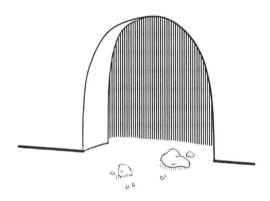

To Learn

The ability to learn truly is astounding
To hear
Then to speak
To see
Then to do
That doesn't just happen
The brain and body
Made up of millions of tiny machines
Figure out how to fire
Ballistic chemicals
To create the functions of man
And records the whole thing
For conscious viewing

Some things are learned quick
The mimics and melodies
Some things take time
Precision and perfection
And complexity
And what's new

Are we really carrying knowledge
From generation to generation
I mean
How much knowledge can be held in a
Collective consciousness
And how much slips out

Or is argued over
Is there anything at all
That everyone can know
Other than what we can learn from instinct
It's the institution
And the culture
Not the brain
That remembers
So it is of utmost importance
That we create an institution
That can account for
Everybody's
Knowledge

Otherwise people are forgotten
And suffering gets silenced

I think the world can be a bit slow sometimes
We have a long way to go
But there's potential
If there's one thing humanity has proven
It's that if we can just get
A spark to fly
Our fires will burn bright

We can learn

HEY

Weeks go by the days fade away
I say this because it takes time for thoughts to grow into
words

A chance encounter fails to fruit
A conversation closes
Nay to say to the word
Hey

Where do the people go
What do the people do

I remember the old lady on the street

How did she live her life
Who were the people she met
How many people did she not get
To say goodbye to

So I say hey
And the line is dead

THE VOID IS NOT A VOID

The void is a creature
That is made up of all greedy desire
It takes and it grows
And everyone has their own monster to face

A wise man once coined it a tale of two wolves
But everyone's got their own metaphor
The only way to keep good alive
Is to choke out that void of desire

Because it is endless
And it will not stop on its own
Appeasement won't work
This is a war

It can corrupt anything
From food to fears
Love and lust
But what's worse is what it creates

Neediness and greed
Self-doubt and selfishness
It'll turn a man into a fool
But if you can tame it

It can become a tool

It's hunger boundless
Means that if you can give it a healthy diet
It can become less unruly
The void can be on your side

But you have to let go
You can't believe it to be omnipotent
It's just a part of a whole
It's been said before but

The hardest fights we often face are the ones that take place
inside of us

ONE FOR MY MOM

Lover of live music
Excellent employer
Amazing artist
Hella cool Hellraiser

Another for Mother

We're high strung
We smoke too much
We can't sleep
Especially when we have to get up early
We like to sing rock and roll
We think everyone's dumb
We think nature's cool
And we're eccentric as balls
We got a strong sweet tooth
We'll skip the table for the booth
We have to be in charge
And like the idea of living large
We like to wear only black
And we'll probably die by heart attack

We're family

Everything Happens for a Reason

Like a leaf in a tornado
A cup of water in the tsunami
You believe everything happens for a reason
But you lose a lot with that kind of letting go

Reason is a choice we make
When we decide what's real
The things that happen around us
Are reflected in the actions we choose

Inward reflection and outward scanning
Don't get lost reasoning for everything
Find the path you're on
And choose where you want to leave footsteps

THE VIEW FROM THE MOUNTAIN SIDE

There's snow beneath me
As I take in the breathtaking view
A cool light fog hangs in the air
I can see clouds bellow

The trees stand tall
I see them between my feet
But the view that takes it all
Is straight ahead

I see another mountain
Far taller
Far steeper
Than the one I'm on

Earth-shattering
The sharp greys
The trees dotting life
The vast wall before me

Nature still holds triumphant over mankind
It's awesome power
It's limitless peaks
Man is but a mite

Witness thee the power of a God

UNTITLED

They say actions speak louder than words
So if my written word was what hurt you most
I guess I can find solace in that

A stupid game with no winners

But the participation prize was pretty good

UNTITLED

A mistake makes mistakes
And the fighter fights
The bitch bellows
And the carrier cries

Can he do the right thing
Is he strong enough
Will the words mean something
Can he pick himself up

The edge of the cliff is where all the best views tempt the tired

March 16, 2020

I'm at the pool but I'm alone in the bleachers
The staff are cleaning and I am thinking
There's a trainee on deck learning
She's kinda cute

If I'd half a mind I'd be cute back

In fact I'd have half the mind to write a poem

The lifeguard by the pool

Oh lifeguard by the pool
Will you throw me your lifesaver
I'd like to win your favour
In an act not so cool

A poem written on my phone
A Monday morning in a quarantined land
I'm sure it's not fun to be a drone
I must be clean, the pool will demand

This would sound better if I had a lute
but I must profess I think you're cute
But I don't know who you are
From my seat, so far

Anyways I didn't have too much to say
I hope you have a wonderful day
One last word if I may
Your hair shines as beautiful as a sunray

CPSIA information can be obtained
at www.ICGtesting.com
Printed in the USA
BVHW072131081021
618498BV00002B/3